LIFE IN THE COUNTRY

LIFE IN THE COUNTRY

With Quotations by
JANE AUSTEN

and Silhouettes by her Nephew
JAMES EDWARD AUSTEN-LEIGH

Edited by FREYDIS JANE WELLAND *and* EILEEN SUTHERLAND
Contributions by MAGGIE LANE *and* JOAN RAY
Afterword by JOAN AUSTEN-LEIGH

THE BRITISH LIBRARY

Dedicated to Joan and Denis
with gratitude and love

ACKNOWLEDGEMENTS
With appreciation to Damaris Jane Brix, Sally Brown, and Carol Shields for their early encouragement;
Eileen Sutherland, Joan Ray, Robert Reid and Maggie Lane for their inspiration, practical contributions and kindnesses;
Anne Giardini, David Way, Keiko Parker, Jim Munro, Bruce Ubukata and Pam Wagner for their thoughtful advice;
Marsha Huff, Neil Wilkie, Sue Hughes, Ewa Lupin, Ben Welland, Bobby Birchall and George Justice for their
ready help, enthusiasm and artistry; to Michael Welland especially for his sensible and amusing support;
and to Janeites everywhere for their enjoyment of all things Jane, including the 'light, bright and sparkling'.

First published 2005 by A Room of One's Own Press
© 2005 A Room of One's Own Press
© 2008 in this edition, The British Library Board
This edition first published 2008 by
The British Library
96 Euston Road
London NW1 2DB
www.bl.uk

British Library Cataloguing in Publication Data
A CIP record for this book is available from The British Library

ISBN 978 0 7123 4985 7

Designed by Robert R. Reid
Printed in Hong Kong by South Sea International Press

Contents

Preface

These delightful silhouettes have brought pleasure to James Edward Austen-Leigh's family for generations. The creamy sheets and patina of the original leather album speak of the time that has passed since the silhouettes were first created. Yet they retain the same freshness, vigour and charm that make Jane Austen's writings so engaging still. On looking through the attractive album of silhouettes, resonances of her novels, letters and charades come to mind.

Jane Austen and her nephew James Edward were united by a particular bond of affection that endeared them to each other and strengthened the ties of family and friendship between them. Their mutual interest in writing was an inspiration to Jane's nieces, and as growing children, they too began writing novels to show to their beloved aunt Jane.

As a young man at Winchester and Oxford, Edward Austen (as he was known then) developed his talent for drawing. Jane said in a letter to his sister Caroline, written from Chawton in 1817: *"We were quite happy to see Edward, it was an unexpected pleasure, & he makes himself as agreeable as ever, sitting in such a quiet comfortable way making his delightful little Sketches."*

He later brought the fine art of silhouettes to perfection, creating wonderfully evocative images of landscapes and the creatures that lived there. His renditions were so accurately shaped that the children could identify each individual dog in a hunting scene.

James Edward made these exquisite silhouettes in the mid-1830s for the amusement of his children, who must have enjoyed discovering the charming details–the quail peeking out from the leafy branch, the fish catching dinner and the dog teasing the cat.

Decades later in *A Memoir of Jane Austen* James Edward Austen-Leigh, then Vicar of Bray, lovingly recollects family gatherings enlivened by Jane's ready wit. As a younger man, he had written a poem *To the Memory of Miss Jane Austen:*

> *Teeming with mimic Life was found*
> *Each offspring of thy Quill:*
> *Though fell the Scene on Fiction's ground,*
> *T'was Nature's Shadow still.*
> *In humble Life's untrodden Vale*
> *T'was thy delight to stray…*

Jane Austen did not live long enough to see James Edward's skillfully created silhouettes, and in this slim volume we fit her exquisite prose to his finely honed art with a sense of pleasure at the way the one reflects the other with engaging insight, irony and humour.

We hope this little book, with its evocative nuances, brings much enjoyment in the scenes and quotations depicted here. Jane Austen's lively text and James Edward's astute observations of nature combine in a way that uniquely illustrates their perspectives on life in the English countryside. As Jane Austen said, to "look upon verdure is the most perfect refreshment."

Freydis Jane Welland & Eileen Sutherland

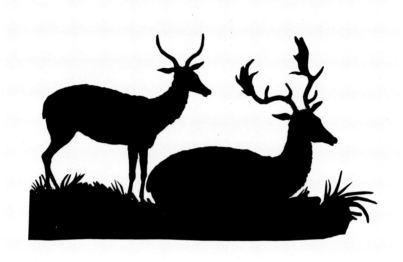

Jane Austen and her family

AMONG the glories of English literature, surely only Shakespeare can match Jane Austen in her power both to delight generations of ordinary readers and to engage the interest of academic ones. She is accessible, inexhaustible, timeless and placeless. This is all the more amazing in that her novels are located very precisely in time and place. Part of her appeal is the picture she portrays, with the most economical of touches, of a vanished and almost quaint society. But it is not mere escapism or yearning for a more ordered moral world that account for her enduring popularity. It is also the wit and humour of her vision, the subtlety of her psychological insight, and the truth to nature of her characters. Above all, perhaps, the snap and sparkle of the writing itself. When we reread Jane Austen, it is with the same thrill of anticipation with which we read favourite poetry, savouring the familiar sequence of words.

But it is futile to try to analyse her hold over her devoted readership, for perhaps everyone has their own reason for falling under her spell. More profitable, perhaps, to ask who was this extraordinarily gifted woman, of little formal education, who published anonymously, was unconnected with any literary movement in her time, yet was perhaps the greatest female genius who ever created fiction. Her name never appeared in print before her death (when a brother wrote a short biographical notice to preface her two posthumously published novels). She was personally known to no other writer, was unfêted by her publisher, and had only her family with whom to discuss the craft of writing.

But what a family. It seems to have supplied all her emotional and intellectual needs. Born in December 1775, she was the seventh of eight children of the Rector of Steventon in Hampshire, the Reverend George Austen and his wife Cassandra Leigh. Growing up in a lively, intelligent household, she enjoyed both the comings and goings of brothers and the constant companionship of her one sister, a true soulmate. She had an assured place in the local social hierarchy, while the wider ramifications of her parents' respective families, with their various landowning, academic and professional strands, gave her a sense of embeddedness in English society at large. Well-travelled in the southern counties of England, from Kent to Devon, from Hampshire to Warwickshire, she knew London well and Bath even better, at a time when Bath was on the cusp between fashionable spa and genteel retirement town. She was familiar with the naval ports of Portsmouth and Southampton, and in the opening years of the nineteenth century she was among the earliest visitors to the string of seaside resorts, lately developed from fishing villages, along the south coast.

The make-up of her family could almost have been designed to bring her the array of ideas and experiences necessary to nurture her talent and her knowledge of the world. One brother, having been adopted by rich relatives, was a wealthy landowner, and gave her entrée into country house society. Another brother was a London banker and afforded her visits to the capital and business acumen to deal with publishers. Two brothers were in Nelson's Royal Navy, bringing the subjects of war, slavery and empire into her ken.

Her eldest brother, whom she acknowledged to be "good and clever," was a clergyman with literary aspirations, editing a magazine at university and writing poetry all his life. James passed on his writing gene to all three of his children, Anna, James Edward and Caroline, and it was in letters to the two elder ones that Jane Austen's few extant observations on the art of fiction were made.

JANE AUSTEN had begun writing at an early age to amuse her family. They were all interested in fiction—"novel readers and not ashamed of being so" in her own words—but the fiction being published in the 1780s and 90s was absurdly unrealistic. The child Jane wrote to burlesque the literary fashions of her day, using the devices of exaggeration and bathos. It is remarkable that what she wrote between the ages of twelve and sixteen should still have the power to make us laugh out loud. We no longer have the models that she was mocking in our minds, but no matter, her jokes are still exceedingly funny. To compare Jane Austen's juvenilia with that of any other major writer is to see an astonishing difference. Most clever children who write are over-earnest, and one would hardly read their efforts for pleasure. It is very different with Jane Austen. The voice that she finds as a child has extraordinary maturity and sophistication without a drop of sententiousness.

By the age of twenty-one, she had written the first versions of three of the major novels in the English canon: *Sense and Sensibility*, *Pride and Prejudice* and *Northanger Abbey*. (The manuscripts are lost, and the extent of later revision is not known.) She made two separate attempts to publish: in 1798 her father offered the manuscript of *First Impressions*, forerunner of *Pride and Prejudice* to a publisher, but it was turned down sight unseen. In 1803 she seemed to be nearer publication when another firm paid her £10 for the manuscript of *Susan*, which was to become *Northanger Abbey* but though he advertised it as forthcoming, he changed his mind and it never appeared.

Not surprisingly, she seems to have suffered some loss of heart. A new novel, known to us as *The Watsons*, was begun and abandoned. By now she was living in Bath, her parents having given up the country rectory where she had spent the first twenty-five years of her existence, and when her father died at the beginning of 1805 her life became even more unsettled, moving with her mother and sister from one set of lodgings to another and suffering the inevitable financial insecurities of women without money of their own (they lived on charity from the Austen brothers). There were also, it would seem, two unsatisfactory romantic episodes: a suitor who died and another whose proposal she first accepted and then, the next morning, in horrible embarrassment, declined.

But in 1809 the richest of the brothers, Edward Knight (he had taken the name of his wealthy benefactors) was able to provide his mother and sisters with a settled home in the shape of Chawton Cottage near Alton in Hampshire, and here the second burst of astonishing creativity took place, begin-

Watercolour of Chawton Cottage.

ning with revision of the manuscripts in hand. *Sense and Sensibility* was published in 1811. "No indeed, I am never too busy to think of *S&S*," she wrote to her sister Cassandra. "I can no more forget it, than a mother can forget her sucking child." She used the same terminology when *Pride and Prejudice* was published two years later. "I want to tell you that I have got my own darling child from London," adding, of Elizabeth Bennet, "I must confess that I think her as delightful a creature as ever appeared in print, & how I shall be able to tolerate those who do not like her, at least, I do not know."

In the remaining four years of life left to her, she wrote three further novels: *Mansfield Park, Emma* and *Persuasion*. To aficionados of her work, there is a subtle difference in tone between the three Steventon, and three Chawton novels. Writing in her thirties at the very height of her powers, she has complete command over her material, while age and experience have brought an accession of tenderness and sympathy towards her people. Her vision is still comic, but it is both more chequered with light and shade, and more profound. *Persuasion*, though ostensibly finished, and certainly full of beauties, was never passed by its author for publication, and there is reason to suppose she might have revised and expanded it had she continued in health. But her health failed, and she turned instead to a new work, *Sanditon*, set in an imaginary seaside resort. Only a few chapters had been drafted when she died in July 1817, aged 41.

Besides her powers as a novelist, she had great gifts of expression as a letter-writer. To read her collected letters, most but by no means all of them addressed to Cassandra, is to journey with her from carefree youth, through the difficulties and satisfactions of her twenties and thirties to sickness and premature death faced with all the resignation she could muster. It is to relish her wit, understand her opinions, and admire her philosophy. It is also to become acquainted with that most supportive and stimulating of extended families, the Austens.

Maggie Lane

The Silhouette Art of James Edward Austen-Leigh

I T IS, perhaps with appropriate irony—given that the silhouettes we are presenting were cut freehand by James Edward Austen-Leigh (1798-1874), the favourite nephew of Jane Austen, whose novels are acclaimed for, among many brilliancies, their exquisite use of irony—that this exquisite art form, requiring considerable manual dexterity, is named after Étienne de Silhouette (1709-1767), French author and politician noted for his tight-fisted financial policies, whose hobby was cutting shadow portraits. Although Monsieur de Silhouette would be an Austen character in the vein of General Tilney or John Dashwood, the art form that is named after him is known for its delicate and simple beauty.

Shadow portraits were cut in Europe as early as 600 B.C. By the 1750s the art of silhouettes had become a frequent pastime in England, especially among aristocrats. The Princess Elizabeth, fourth daughter of King George III, was an avid amateur artist who cut and painted silhouettes of the Royal Family. Silhouette posing and cutting were soon popular in fashionable drawing-rooms. As this passion for silhouettes grew and the price of scissors decreased by the 1820s, amateur silhouette artists came from many more walks of life.

The easiest way to create a silhouette, of course, is to have one's subject pose in light to form a shadow and then trace the profile. The popular silhouette of Jane Austen known as "L'aimable Jane," is a hollow-cut silhouette made in that way—by tracing the profile on white paper, cutting out the profile, and placing this hollow image on paper. However, the more deft handler of scissors and better artist can cut silhouettes without tracing shadows. James Edward Austen-Leigh was such an artist.

The only son of Jane Austen's eldest brother James, Edward—as he was called—demonstrated artistic talent from boyhood. According to his daughter, Mary Augusta, in *James Edward Austen-Leigh, A Memoir*: "As a boy he had been accustomed to cut out and paint

Caroline Austen

packs of hounds, printing their names on the blank side, and the first time his sister Caroline, when a little girl, saw a real pack of hounds assembled, she ran around to look for their names on their other sides." Young Caroline's charming reaction to the hunting hounds attests to the realism of Edward's youthful silhouette artistry, which continued into his adulthood.

Recounting *Family Games and Charades* in the *Memoir*, Mary Augusta writes: "In the winter evenings he would exercise the same kind of talent he had shown in cutting out

Mary Augusta Austen-Leigh

groups from sheets of black paper, and would produce packs of hounds with hunters, foxes, and hares, first outlined on drawing paper, then painted the proper colours, and finally cut out, so that by a little separation of their feet, they could be made to stand up." His younger children—Edward and his wife Emma had ten children—who had been sent to bed earlier in the evening, would run downstairs the next morning to see "what additions to the pack might have appeared in their absence on the drawing room mantelpiece, where the hounds were set up when finished."

William Chute, M.P.

Mary Augusta continues: "A pack when completed could be arranged on a long piece of green baize, which was provided with fences, and made a very good hunting field. They were beautifully executed and … show their author's power of eye and hand, and perfect knowledge of his subject. No two hounds were alike, many being reproductions of hounds he had known well in The Vine and H. H. packs more than twenty years earlier. The name of every hound was written on the blank side. Our mother used to wish they could be reproduced in metal, as being more durable than drawing paper. They were certainly delicate little creatures for children's play things."

The Vyne Hunt that Mary Augusta mentions played an important part in Edward's

Mrs. Chute of The Vyne

Speen, 1844.

life. Mr. and Mrs. William John Chute of The Vyne, Hampshire, were close friends and neighbours of his parents and grandparents for many years. Indeed, Edward knew the Chutes from his earliest childhood. Mr. Chute (1757-1827) was M.P. for Hampshire (1790-1806) and Master of The Vyne Hunt, with which, along with other packs, Edward hunted two or three times weekly, especially during his curacy of Newton, near Burghclere, Berkshire. (He had been ordained in 1823). "His mother used to say how glad she was that Edward should hunt, as he brought her back all the news of the neighbourhood." During this period, Edward was "an enthusiastic fisherman, having been instructed in the art by his uncle" on his mother's side, the Rev. Fulwar Craven Fowle of Kintbury, who incidentally was the brother of Cassandra Austen's fiancé, Thomas.

Possibly another, even stronger, attraction for Edward at The Vyne was Emma Smith (1801-1876), one of Mrs. Chute's nieces, the second of six daughters of her younger sister Augusta Smith. Edward was "a great favourite" with Mr. and Mrs. Chute, and all the Smiths regarded The Vyne as "almost a second home … from their infancy." Mrs. Chute encouraged the romance between Edward and Emma by "inviting both to stay" at The Vyne. The two were married in 1828.

Edward's knowledge of The Vyne Hunt and Mr. Chute led to his being asked in 1864 by a Hampshire friend "to write down some of his recollections of the Vine Hunt and its founder, Mr. Chute." The result in the following year was *Recollections of The Early Days Of The Vine Hunt And Of Its Founder William John Chute, Esq., Of The Vine Together With Brief Notices Of The Adjoining Hunts,* by A Sexagenarian. Comparing Mr. Chute in church to *The Spectator*'s Sir Roger de Coverley, "giving out the responses in an audible tone, with an occasional glance to see what tenants were at church, and what school children were misbehaving," Edward also observes that "he was devoted to hunting, but he was neither a good rider, nor … a good sportsman…. But his popularity with his field was unbounded; and I have heard it said, 'After all, one would rather have a middling sport with Chute, than better with any one else'."

Recollections is filled with details of The Vyne and other hunts that only an avid hunter and sportsman would know. Thus it is not surprising that the majority of the silhouettes in this volume show outdoor country life, created during a period in the mid 1830s, when a throat ailment compelled Edward to take a sabbatical from his clerical life and sporting pastimes—both of which he loved—and remain indoors at the family's new home in Speen, Berkshire. As Mary Augusta comments in the *Memoir* of her father, "His great natural activity, both of mind and body, must have made this long season of enforced idleness particularly trying." To make the best use of this time, Edward taught all his young sons and prepared them so well that three of them won honours at Eton and accolades later in life.

"He also took to a new occupation, which he carried to great perfection. This was cutting out figures and scenes from natural life in black paper.... He was taught this art by Miss Clinton—a relation of Mr. [Henry] Majendie, Vicar of Speen [and the chief clerical friend our father ever possessed]— who came to visit at the vicarage. He never drew his pictures, but cut them out by eye, and they are wonderful for their accuracy, grace, variety, and observation of nature. I never saw or heard of any like them. Miss Clinton's were confined to a few half-classical figures, but our father took his subject from natural objects. He used special scissors, the points being about an inch long, and the curved handles about three inches. These and a sheet of black paper were his only tools. A few of his groups were placed on screens or a cabinet of white wood, but the greater number are preserved in a book."

Edward created his most artful silhouettes, cut freehand, and predominantly of outdoor scenes of country life, during a period when he had to remain indoors. On the following pages are many of the silhouettes that appear in the book Mary Augusta mentions. In the late 1860s, for his eldest grandson, Edward painted and cut out his last pack of hounds, "with fingers that had in no way lost their cunning."

Joan Klingel Ray

Silhouette by Miss Clinton

"I hope, my dear," said Mr. Bennet to his wife, as they were at breakfast the next morning, "that you have ordered a good dinner to-day, because I have reason to expect an addition to our family party."

MRS. BENNET: Good lord! How unlucky! There is not a bit of fish to be got today.

Pride and Prejudice, Volume I, Chapter 2.

Darcy had never been so bewitched by any woman as he was by her.

But Elizabeth, who had not the least inclination to remain with them, laughingly answered, "No, no; stay where you are. You are charmingly group'd, and appear to uncommon advantage. The picturesque would be spoilt by admitting a fourth."

Pride and Prejudice, Volume I, Chapter 10.

… a very kind and careful guardian …

Pride and Prejudice, Volume I, Chapter 16.

*Elizabeth has the unexpected happiness of an invitation
from her aunt and uncle Gardiner to join them on a tour of pleasure.*

ELIZABETH BENNET: "My dear, dear aunt," she rapturously cried, "what delight! What felicity!…What are men to rocks and mountains? Oh! What hours of transport we shall spend!"

Pride and Prejudice, Volume II, Chapter 4.

*Elizabeth Bennet and Maria Lucas are staying at Hunsford Parsonage
with Mr Collins and his amiable Charlotte:*

About the middle of the next day ... a sudden noise below seemed to speak the whole house in confusion; and after listening a moment she heard somebody running up stairs in a violent hurry, and calling loudly after her. She opened the door and met Maria in the landing place.... Down they ran into the dining-room, which fronted the lane, in quest of this wonder; it was two ladies stopping in a low phaeton at the garden gate. "And is this all?" cried Elizabeth. "I expected at least that the pigs were got into the garden, and here it is nothing but Lady Catherine and her daughter!"

Pride and Prejudice, Volume II, Chapter 5.

The Gardiners and Elizabeth are walking in the grounds of Pemberley.

Their progress was slow, for Mr. Gardiner, though seldom able to indulge the taste, was very fond of fishing, and was so much engaged in watching the occasional appearance of some trout in the water, and talking to the man about them, that he advanced but little.

Pride and Prejudice, Volume III, Chapter 1.

Mr. Darcy meets Elizabeth and the Gardiners beside a stream at Pemberley.

The conversation soon turned upon fishing and Elizabeth heard Mr. Darcy invite him, with the greatest civility, to fish there as often as he chose, while he continued in the neighbourhood, offering at the same time to supply him with fishing tackle, and pointing out those parts of the stream where there was usually most sport.

Pride and Prejudice, Volume III, Chapter 1.

JOHN DASHWOOD: It was my father's request to me … that I should assist his widow and daughters…. One had rather, on such occasions, do too much than too little.

FANNY DASHWOOD: I am convinced within myself that your father had no idea of your giving them any money at all. The assistance he thought of, I dare say, was only … sending them presents of fish and game, and so forth, whenever they are in season.

Sense and Sensibility, Volume I, Chapter 2.

As a house, Barton Cottage, though small, was comfortable and compact; but as a cottage it was defective, for the building was regular, the roof was tiled, the window shutters were not painted green, nor were the walls covered with honeysuckles.

Sense and Sensibility, Volume I, Chapter 6.

Marianne Dashwood, out for a walk with her sister Margaret, falls and sprains her ankle.

A gentleman carrying a gun, with two pointers playing round him, was passing up the hill, and within a few yards of Marianne, when her accident happened. He put down his gun and ran to her assistance.

Sense and Sensibility, Volume I, Chapter 9.

Colonel Brandon tells Elinor about the orphaned Eliza:
Our ages were nearly the same, and from our earliest years we
were playfellows and friends. I cannot remember the time when
I did not love Eliza.

Sense and Sensibility, Volume II, Chapter 9.

The good understanding between the Colonel and Miss Dashwood seemed rather to declare the honours of the mulberry-tree, the canal and the yew arbour, would all be made over to *her*.

Sense and Sensibility, Volume II, Chapter 10.

Marianne Dashwood is beginning to plan again, to the delight of her sister Elinor:

MARIANNE: "When the weather is settled, and I have recovered my strength," said she, "we will take long walks together every day…. We will often go to the old ruins of the Priory, and try to trace its foundations as far as we are told they once reached."

Sense and Sensibility, Volume III, Chapter 10.

Willoughby is married and settled at Combe Magna.

He lived to exert, and frequently to enjoy himself ....
In his breed of horses and dogs, and in sporting of
every kind, he found no inconsiderable degree of
domestic felicity.

Sense and Sensibility, Volume III, Chapter 14.

*Catherine Morland was to be the chosen visitor
of the Tilneys at Northanger Abbey.*

Her passion for ancient edifices was next to her passion for Henry Tilney, and castles and abbies made usually the charm of those reveries which his image did not fill. To see and explore either the ramparts and keep of one, or the cloisters of the other, had been for many weeks a darling wish.

Northanger Abbey, Volume II, Chapter 2.

Catherine Morland is visiting Henry Tilney's parsonage at Woodston,
and exclaims at the view from one window:

Oh! what a sweet little cottage there is among the trees—apple trees too! It is the prettiest cottage!

GENERAL TILNEY: You like it—you approve it as an object;—it is enough. Henry, remember that Robinson is spoken to about it. The cottage remains.

Northanger Abbey, Volume II, Chapter 11.

LORD OSBORNE: A woman never looks better than on horseback.

EMMA: But every woman may not have the inclination, or the means.

LORD OSBORNE: I fancy Miss Watson, when once they had the inclination, the means w^d soon follow.

EMMA: Your Lordship thinks we always have our own way.... Female economy will do a great deal my Lord, but it cannot turn a small income into a large one.

The Watsons.

My hounds will be hunting this Country next week—I beleive they will throw off at Stanton wood on Wednesday at 9 o'clock. I mention this in hopes of y^r being drawn out to see what is going on. If the morning's tolerable, pray do us the honour of giving us your good wishes in person.

The Watsons.

But the chief beauty of Steventon consisted in its hedgerows. A hedgerow, in that country, does not mean a thin formal line of quickset, but an irregular border of copse-wood and timber, often wide enough to contain within it a winding foot-path, or a rough cart track. Under its shelter the earliest primroses, anemones, and wild hyacinths were to be found; sometimes, the first bird's-nest; and, now and then, the unwelcome adder.

J. E. Austen-Leigh, *A Memoir of Jane Austen*, Chapter 2.

I shall order a Barrel of oysters, & be famously snug.

The Watsons.

... the new mare proved a treasure ...

Mansfield Park, Volume I, Chapter 4.

Mary Crawford discusses the conveyance of her harp with Edmund Bertram:

MARY: Not by a wagon or cart; Oh! No, nothing of that kind could be hired in the village…. Guess my surprise, when I found that I had been asking the most unreasonable, most impossible thing in the world, had offended all the farmers, all the labourers, all the hay in the parish.

Mansfield Park, Volume I, Chapter 6.

Sir Thomas Bertram's attention is diverted from the Theatricals at Mansfield Park by his son:

TOM BERTRAM: We have had such incessant rains almost since October began, that we have been nearly confined to the house for days together. I have hardly taken out a gun since the 3rd. Tolerable sport the first three days, but there has been no attempting any thing since. The first day I went over Mansfield Wood, and Edmund took the copses beyond Easton, and we brought home six brace between us, and might each have killed six times as many; but we respect your pheasants, sir, I assure you, as much as you could desire. I do not think you will find your woods by any means worse stocked than they were. *I* never saw Mansfield Wood so full of pheasants in my life as this year. I hope you will take a day's sport there yourself, sir, soon.

Mansfield Park, Volume II, Chapter 1.

She could not, would not, dared not attempt it.

Mansfield Park, Volume I, Chapter 18.

Fanny muses to Miss Crawford:

If any one faculty of our nature may be called *more* wonderful than the rest, I do think it is memory. There seems something more speakingly incomprehensible in the powers, the failures, the inequalities of memory ... than in any other of our intelligences. The memory is sometimes so retentive, so serviceable, so obedient—at others so bewildered.... We are to be sure a miracle in every way, but our powers of recollecting and of forgetting do seem peculiarly past finding out.

Mansfield Park, Volume II, Chapter 4.

With spirits, courage, and curiosity up to anything, William expressed an inclination to hunt; and Crawford could mount him without the slightest inconvenience to himself. [Fanny] feared for William; by no means convinced by all that he could relate of his own horsemanship in various countries, of the scrambling parties in which he had been engaged, the rough horses and mules he had ridden, or his many narrow escapes from dreadful falls, that he was at all equal to the management of a high-fed hunter in an English fox-chase; nor till he returned safe and well... could she feel any of that obligation to Mr. Crawford for lending the horse which he had fully intended it should produce.

Mansfield Park, Volume II, Chapter 6.

... all serenity and satisfaction ...

Mansfield Park, Volume I, Chapter 14.

... the happy flutter ...

Mansfield Park, Volume II, Chapter 9.

Anne has just arrived at Sir Walter's house in Camden-Place
when a knock is heard at the door. Mr. Elliot is ushered in.

He staid an hour with them. The elegant little clock on the mantle-piece had struck 'eleven with its silver sounds,' and the watchman was beginning to be heard at a distance telling the same tale, before Mr. Elliot or any of them seemed to feel that he had been there long.

Persuasion, Volume II, Chapter 3.

Anne Elliot is visiting her sister Mary at Uppercross.

MARY MUSGROVE: Charles is out shooting. I have not seen him since seven o'clock. He would go…. He said he should not stay out long; but he has never come back.

Anne could believe … that a woman of real understanding might have given more consequence to his character, and more usefulness, rationality, and elegance to his habit and pursuits. As it was, he did nothing with much zeal, but sport.

Persuasion, Volume I, Chapters 5 & 6.

Imagination is everything.

Letter to Cassandra, Steventon, Saturday, 17 November 1798.

… to form a cool and impartial opinion, and prepare his objections on a fairer gound than inequality of situations.

Northanger Abbey, Volume II, Chapter 11.

CHLOE:
I go to Town
And when I come down,
I shall be married to Stree-phon
And that to me will be fun.

CHORUS:
Be fun, be fun, be fun,
And that to me will be fun.

Song, First Act of a Comedy.

Another world must be unfurled,
Another language known.

Panegyric on a Young Friend.

Heaven forbid that I should ever offer such encouragement to Explanations, as to give a clear one on any occasion myself.

Letter to Cassandra, 13 Queen's Square, Bath, Friday, 17 May 1799.

Follies and nonsense, whims and inconsistencies do divert me
I own, and I laugh at them whenever I can.

Pride and Prejudice, Volume I, Chapter 11.

Her charm to children was great sweetness of manner; she seemed to love you, and you loved her naturally in return.... Soon came the delight of her playful talk. Everything she could make amusing to a child ... she would tell us the most delightful stories, chiefly of Fairyland, and her Fairies had all characters of their own. The tale was invented ... on the spur of the moment, and was sometimes continued for two or three days.

Personal Aspects of Jane Austen, M. A. Austen-Leigh.

… after having walked about a mile and a half we sate down by the side of a clear limpid stream to refresh our exhausted limbs. The place was suited to meditation. A grove of full-grown Elms sheltered us from the East…. Before us ran the murmuring brook…. We were in a mood for contemplation.

Love and Freindship, Letter the 13th.

Your kind anxiety … was as much thrown away as kind anxiety usually is.

Letter to Cassandra, Lyme, Friday, 14 September 1804.

The Overton Scotchman has been kind enough to rid me of some of my money, in exchange for six shifts and four pair of stockings.

Letter to Cassandra, Steventon, 25 November 1798.

… with what happy feelings of Escape!

Letter to Cassandra, Godmersham, Thursday, 30 June 1808.

In the meantime for Elegance & Ease & Luxury ... I shall
eat Ice and drink French wine, & be above vulgar Economy.

Letter to Cassandra, Godmersham, Thursday, 30 June 1808.

We have felt, we do feel, for you all—as you will not need to be told—for you, for Fanny, for Henry, for Lady Bridges, & for dearest Edward, whose loss and whose sufferings seem to make those of every other person nothing.—God be praised! that you can say what you do of him—that he has a religious Mind to bear him up, & a Disposition that will gradually lead him to comfort.

Letter to Cassandra, Castle Square, Southampton, 13 October 1808.

While I write now, George is most industriously making and naming paper ships, at which he afterwards shoots with horse-chestnuts, brought from Steventon on purpose.

Letter to Cassandra, Castle Square, Southampton, Monday, 24 October 1808.

The chicken are all alive and fit for the table, but we save them for something grand.

Letter to Cassandra, Chawton, Wednesday, 29 May 1811.

Edward … would rather not be asked to go anywhere.… I read him the cheif of your letter.… Your finding so much comfort from his Cows gave him evident pleasure.

Letter to Cassandra, Godmersham Park, 23–24 September 1813.

Oh, what a Henry!

Letter to Cassandra, Chawton, Thursday, 23 June 1814.

He was a piece of Perfection, noisy Perfection himself,
which I always recollect with regard.

Letter to Francis Austen, Chawton, 3 July 1813.

... very much the gentleman ... and, poor man! is so totally deaf that they say he could not hear a cannon, were it fired close to him; having no cannon at hand to make the experiment, I took it for granted, and talked to him a little with my fingers.... I recommended him to read....

Letter to Cassandra, Castle Square, Southampton, Tuesday, 27 December 1808.

We quite run over with books…. I am reading a book …
which I find delightfully written & highly entertaining. I am
… much in love with the author—the first soldier I ever
sighed for—but he does write with extraordinary force &
spirit.

Letter to Cassandra, Chawton, Sunday even'g, 24 January 1813.

They were late because they did not set out earlier, and did not allow time enough.

Letter to Cassandra, Godmersham Park, Thursday, 14 October 1813.

My Mother's wood is brought in, but, by some mistake, no bavins. She must therefore buy some.

Letter to Cassandra, Chawton, Thursday, 23 June 1814.

… this exquisite weather.… I enjoy it all over me, from top to toe, from right to left, Longitudinally, Perpendicularly, Diagonally … nice, unwholesome, Unseasonable, relaxing, close, muggy weather!

Letter to Cassandra, Hans Place, London, 2 December 1815.

Give our love to the little Boys, if they can be persuaded to remember us.

Letter to Alethea Bigg, Chawton, Friday, 24 January 1817.

Only think of your lost Dormouse being brought back to you!
I was quite astonished.

Letter to Caroline, Chawton, Thursday, 23 January 1817.

… availing himself of the precious opportunity …

Emma, Volume I, Chapter 15.

The low French windows of the Drawing room commanded the road & all the Paths across the Down.

Sanditon, Chapter 7.

When Winchester races first took their beginning …
The races however were fix'd and determin'd
The company met & the weather was charming

Venta. A poem written at Winchester on Tuesday, 15 July 1817.

You may lie on my first, by the side of a stream,
And my second compose to the Nymph you adore,
But if, when you've none of my whole, her esteem
And affection diminish—think of her no more!

Riddle.

I was very much pleased with the country in general.

Letter to Cassandra, Sloane Street, London, 20 May 1813.

James Edward Austen-Leigh

AFTERWORD by JOAN AUSTEN-LEIGH

Joan Austen-Leigh, acclaimed playwright and novelist and co-founder of the Jane Austen Society of North America, was for many years editor of the Society's journal Persuasions. *Together with her family, Joan Austen-Leigh gave Jane Austen's writing desk into the care of The British Library, turning a cherished private heritage into public memories for generations to come.*

James Edward Austen-Leigh

"More than half a century has passed away since I, the youngest of the mourners, attended the funeral of my dear aunt Jane in Winchester Cathedral...."

SO WROTE MY GREAT-GRANDFATHER, James Edward Austen-Leigh, the favourite nephew of his aunt. Little did he suspect that his words would come down to posterity—that in a hundred years' time not only would Jane Austen's novels still be being read, but also his own loving, gracious, evocative *Memoir*.

James Edward (always known as Edward) was the son of Jane's eldest brother, the Reverend James Austen and his second wife Mary (née Lloyd) Austen. Edward had a unique bond with his aunt: both had been born and lived the first twenty-five years of their lives at Steventon Rectory. Be that as it may, the *Memoir's* elegant prose, as easy to read as any modern biography,

Steventon Rectory, taken from a scrapbook compiled by J. E. Austen-Leigh about 1835.

paints not only its subject, so that we seem to see Jane Austen living and breathing before us, but also a lively portrait of English country life of the period. Familiar with this as we may think we are, through the families we have come to know at Mansfield Park and Rosings, Barton Cottage and Hartfield, to read the *Memoir* is to comprehend at first hand the manners and customs of day-to-day life as actually experienced and vividly recalled by one whose delightful character informs his pages.

This charm caused Edward to be much loved in the family and esteemed even by his headmaster, Dr. Gabell of Winchester, who wrote to Edward's father in 1814: "To the very favourable reports which I have had the pleasure of making to you from time to time on the conduct of your excellent son, I can add nothing."

It was while Edward was still at school that he was let in on the hitherto closely guarded secret—even from her own nephews and nieces—of Jane's authorship. In his surprise and delight he burst into verse:

TO MISS J. AUSTEN

No words can express, my dear Aunt, my surprise
Or make you conceive how I opened my eyes,
Like a pig Butcher Pile has just struck with his knife,
When I heard for the very first time in my life
That I have the honour to have a relation
Whose works were dispersed through the whole of the nation.
I assure you, however, I'm terribly glad;
Oh dear! just to think (and the thought drives me mad)
That dear Mrs Jennings's good-natured strain,
Was really the produce of your witty brain,
That you made the Middletons, Dashwoods and all,
And that you (not young Ferrars) found out that a ball
May be given in cottages never so small.
And though Mr Collins, so grateful for all,
Will Lady de Bourgh his dear Patroness call,
'Tis to your ingenuity really he owed
His living, his wife, and his humble abode.

This news of their aunt's success encouraged both Edward and his sisters, Anna and Caroline, to attempt to write novels of their own, and to badger their ever-patient aunt for criticism and comment. It is in a letter to Edward that the most famous description of her work exists. She learned that a portion of the story he was writing had been lost:

"Two chapters & a half to be missing is monstrous! It is well that *I* have not been at Steventon lately, & therefore cannot be suspected of purloining them;—two strong twigs & a half towards a Nest of my own, would have been something.—I do not think however that any theft of that sort would be really very useful to me. What should I do with your strong, manly, spirited Sketches, full of Variety and Glow?—How could I possibly join them on to the little bit (two Inches wide) of Ivory on which I work with so fine a Brush, as produces little effect after much labour?"

Edward was now eighteen, and the mutual affection and regard between nephew and aunt increased with every visit he paid to Chawton. Jane wrote to a friend, Edward "grows still, and still improves in appearance, at least in the estimation of his aunts, who love him better and better, as they see the sweet temper and warm affections of the boy confirmed in the young man."

How could the boy sitting sketching in his aunt's parlour have known that one day he would be called upon to compose her biography?

Describing those distant days, he wrote, "Though in the course of fifty years I have forgotten much, I have not forgotten that Jane Austen was the delight of all her nephews and nieces. We did not think of her as being clever, still less as being famous: but we valued her as one always kind, sympathising, and amusing."

On 18 July 1817 Jane Austen died, followed soon after by her brother James. Edward took orders, much to the chagrin of his great-aunt, Jane Leigh Perrot, who had a dislike of the profession of clergyman. But fortune smiled on the handsome, talented, pleasant young man. In 1828 he married Emma Smith, sister of Sir Charles Smith of Suttons, and niece of Mrs Chute of the Vine in Hampshire. James Edward's family were friends of the Chutes and hunted with Mr Chute's hounds.

Aunt Jane Leigh Perrot was delighted at this good match. When she died

Scarlets, a drawing from the scrapbook of James Edward Austen-Leigh.

in 1836 she left James Edward her handsome house, Scarlets, on condition that he took the name and arms of Leigh. A testimony to that obligation still exists at Scarlets, where the Leigh and Austen coats of arms and the date have been incorporated into a window over the staircase.

Edward now embarked on the exemplary career of a Victorian clergyman. He became the father of a large family, eight sons and two daughters. (Many years later, one of his sons, William, and a grandson, Richard, were to write the definitive *Life and Letters of Jane Austen*.) He built a church and a school near his property. Later, with so many sons to educate, he let Scarlets to a tenant, and moved to Bray, near Windsor and Eton.

During Edward's lifetime, only one new edition of Jane's works had been published, and it seemed as if her reputation, slight as it had been, might fade away entirely. But the enthusiasm of a vast, secret, swelling multitude of new readers would not be denied. Mary Austen-Leigh, daughter of Edward, in *A Memoir* of her father, recalls rather touchingly, "Jane Austen's books appeared to us then, and for a long time afterwards, to be a family and almost a private possession. Our father looked upon it as an accepted fact that to enjoy them required a mind of a peculiar order, and that it was not to be expected that she could ever become a great favourite with the general public.... When, in the course of time, we heard of certain other families who knew and cared for [her] as we did, it came as a surprise, and made us feel that, if we could but meet, we must be friends on the strength of it."

Nevertheless Edward was urged by his family to publish his memories of his aunt. He demurred, he was not in the habit of writing for publication. Yet he habitually preached fifty sermons a year, and in 1865 had published *Recollection of the Early Days of the Vine Hunt*. Finally he was prevailed upon, for he was obliged to concede that "little as I have to tell, there is no one else who could tell as much of her." He began the task. He consulted his sisters. Caroline Austen had transcribed her own recollections two years previously and was willing to help. He travelled to Steventon, where the rectory had now been torn down, he wrote to his cousin Fanny Knatchbull (her son, Lord Brabourne, ultimately edited the first edition of Jane Austen's letters), and after five months' work, appropriately on Jane's birthday, 16 December 1869, the *Memoir* appeared, "by her nephew, J. E. Austen-Leigh, Vicar of Bray, Berks."

To his surprise the edition soon sold out, and a second was required. Mary Augusta Austen-Leigh tells us that "the sum which the two editions brought him amounted, I think, to about £80." Some of this he employed in placing a brass tablet to his aunt's memory in Winchester Cathedral. The tablet, which fills up a recess in the stone panel-work, was designed by Mr. Wyatt, the architect who supervised the restoration of the church at Bray for Rev. James Edward Austen-Leigh.

Fittingly, the highly-polished reflective tablet commemorating Jane Austen as "known to many by her writings, endeared to her family by the varied charms of her character," was placed in her memory at Winchester Cathedral by her favourite nephew.

In one of her last letters, sent from Mrs. Davids in Winchester on May 27, 1817, Jane Austen wrote to him:

> *I know no better way my dearest Edward, of thanking you for your most affectionate concern for me....*
>
> *God bless you my dear Edward.... & may you possess—as I dare say you will—the greatest blessing of all, in the consciousness of not being unworthy of their Love. I could not feel this.*
>
> *Your very affec: Aunt*
>
> *J.A.*

Joan Austen-Leigh, drawn by Ewa Lupin.

Originally published in London in May, 1989, on the occasion of the re-publication of *A Memoir of Jane Austen* by J. E. Austen-Leigh, this article was adapted by Joan Austen-Leigh's eldest daughter Freydis Jane Welland, and reprinted courtesy of the Folio Society.

The Illustrations

THE PORTRAITS

Jane Austen *James Edward Austen-Leigh* *Mary Augusta Austen-Leigh*

THE PORTRAIT OF JANE AUSTEN was the frontispiece for James Edward Austen-Leigh's *Memoir* of Jane Austen. "The memoir was begun on March 20, 1869, and was finished early in September," recalls Mary Augusta Austen-Leigh. "It was thought important that a portrait should appear with it.… His cousin Miss Austen, daughter of Admiral Charles Austen, lent him a small unfinished portrait of Aunt Jane, painted in watercolours by her sister Cassandra. The picture that appears at the beginning of the *Memoir* was painted by Mr. Andrews, an artist then living at Maidenhead, and was based on the sketch by Cassandra. He carried it out under the superintendence and with the advice of our father and his two sisters, and when completed they considered the likeness sufficiently good to justify him in offering it to the public as a portrait of Jane Austen."

SOON AFTER THEIR WEDDING, Edward Austen and his wife Emma sat for their portraits in London. These portraits, painted in oils by Mrs Carpenter in 1829, are among a lifetime of images of James Edward Austen-Leigh which trace the evolution of portrait art from a silhouette of him as a young man at Eton, to photographs and more contemporary portraits of him as an older man. His image is engraved in the stonework of Bray Church.

THEIR DAUGHTER, MARY AUGUSTA AUSTEN-LEIGH, had the "charm of a rare personality" which shines through her portrait and her writings. At the age of 81 she wrote *Personal Aspects of Jane Austen*, a fresh and delicate view of Jane Austen and her family.

CAROLINE AUSTEN, James Edward Austen-Leigh's younger sister, wrote her own *Reminiscences of Jane Austen*. The drawing of her may have been done at Steventon by her Aunt Cassandra, as a keepsake for Edward, who himself made dozens of sketches and silhouettes of his contemporaries.

THE SILHOUETTES

From the Regency period to the mid-1800s, silhouettes were the height of fashion, until their use dwindled with the advent of photography. Many of James Edward Austen-Leigh's silhouettes are published here for the first time, and virtually all are reproduced in actual size. The dimensions of the 120 silhouettes range from 7 x 4¼ inches to 1 x 1½ inches and some are inscribed underneath by Emma (neé Smith) Austen-Leigh. The silhouettes, which are mostly black with occasional reverse silhouettes in white on cream paper, are enclosed in a fine hand-tooled leather album 7½ by 4½ and 1½ inches thick, with delicate cross-hatching and gilt decoration.

CHAWTON COTTAGE

The watercolour of Chawton Cottage, with the little duck pond just visible, is believed to be painted by Anna Lefroy, the eldest daughter of James Austen. In happy anticipation of their life at Chawton, Jane Austen wrote to her brother Frank:

> As for ourselves, we're very well;
> As unaffected prose will tell.—
> Cassandra's pen will paint our state,
> The many comforts that await
> Our Chawton home, how much we find
> Already in it, to our mind;
> And how convinced, that when complete
> It will all other houses beat
> That ever have been made or mended,
> With rooms concise, or rooms distended.
> You'll find us very snug next year …
>
> *Jane Austen, 26 July 1809*

In his *Memoir* James Edward Austen-Leigh speaks of the quiet life at Chawton Cottage where Jane lived with Mrs Austen, Cassandra and their friend Martha Lloyd: "In that well-occupied female party there must have been many precious hours of silence during which the pen was busy at the little mahogany writing desk while Fanny Price, or Emma Woodhouse, or Anne Elliot was growing into beauty and interest."

The painting of Chawton Cottage is courtesy of Damaris Jane Brix.

THE DRAWINGS

Stoneleigh Abbey, September 1833.

All drawings are taken from James Edward Austen-Leigh's scrapbooks.

"IN EACH SUCCEEDING GENERATION, members of my family have written about Jane Austen." So wrote Jane Austen Society of North America co-founder Joan Austen-Leigh. Her own contributions span diverse times and continents: on the bicentenary of Jane Austen's birth she created *Our Own Particular Jane, A Piece of Theatre based on the Life, Letters and Literature of Jane Austen*. "A splendid entertainment" done with "charm, delicate insight and impeccable scholarship," said reviewers. *A Visit to Highbury* and *Later Days at Highbury* are epistolary novels providing another view of *Emma* "almost as light, bright and sparkling as anything Jane Austen wrote."

Bibliography

Jane Austen. *Sense and Sensibility*: A Novel in Three Volumes. By a Lady. London: Printed for the Author and Published by T. Egerton, Whitehall, 1811.

Jane Austen. *Pride and Prejudice*: A Novel. In Three Volumes. By the Author of "Sense and Sensibility." London: Printed for T. Egerton, Whitehall, 1813.

Jane Austen. *Mansfield Park*: A Novel. In Three Volumes. By the Author of "Sense and Sensibility" and "Pride and Prejudice." London: T. Egerton, Whitehall, 1814.

Jane Austen. *Emma*: A Novel. In Three Volumes. By the Author of "Pride and Prejudice" &c. &c. London: Printed for John Murray, 1816.

Jane Austen. *Northanger Abbey*: and *Persuasion*. By the Author of "Pride and Prejudice," "Mansfield Park," &c. With a biographical notice of the author. In Four Volumes. London: John Murray, Albemarle Street, 1818.

Letters of Jane Austen. Edward, Lord Brabourne, ed. 2 vols. London: Richard Bentley and Son, 1884.

Charades, Written a Hundred Years Ago by Jane Austen and Her Family. London: Spottiswoode & Co., 1895.

Jane Austen. *Love and Freindship and Other Early Works now first printed from the original Ms. with a preface by G.K. Chesterton.* London: Chatto & Windus, 1922.

Jane Austen's Letters to her sister Cassandra and others. Collected and ed. R.W. Chapman. 2nd edition. London: Oxford University Press, 1952.

The Novels of Jane Austen. The text based on Collation of the Early Editions by R.W. Chapman in Five Volumes. Third Edition. London, New York, Toronto: Geoffrey Cumberledge, Oxford University Press, Fifth Impression, 1953.

The Works of Jane Austen. Volume VI: Minor Works. Now first collected and edited from the manuscripts by R.W. Chapman, with illustrations from contemporary sources. London, New York, Toronto: Geoffrey Cumberledge, Oxford University Press, 1954.

J. E. Austen. *To the Memory of Miss Jane Austen, Sunday September 28th, 1817*. Poem transcribed from the original by George Holbert Tucker.

James Edward Austen Leigh. *Recollections Of The Early Days of the Vine Hunt and of its founder William John Chute, Esq., M.P. of The Vine together with Brief Notices of the Adjoining Hunts by a Sexagenarian*. London: Spottiswoode & Co., 1865.

James Edward Austen-Leigh. *A Memoir of Jane Austen by her nephew J. E. Austen-Leigh*, Vicar of Bray, Berks. London: Richard Bentley, Publisher in Ordinary to Her Majesty, 1870.

Caroline Austen. *My Aunt Jane Austen, A Memoir*. Winchester: Jane Austen Memorial Trust, new edition 1991 (first printed 1952).

Caroline Austen. *Reminiscences of Caroline Austen*. Introduction by Deirdre Le Faye. Guildford: The Jane Austen Society, 1986.

Mary Augusta Austen Leigh. *James Edward Austen Leigh, A Memoir by his daughter Mary Augusta Austen Leigh*. For private circulation. 1911.

Mary Augusta Austen-Leigh. *Personal Aspects of Jane Austen*. London: John Murray, 1920.

William Austen-Leigh and Richard Arthur Austen-Leigh. *Jane Austen, Her Life and Letters, A Family Record*. London: Smith, Elder & Co., 1913.

Sue McKechnie. *British Silhouette Artists and their Work*. New York: Sotheby, Parke Bernet, 1978.

David Gilson. *A Bibliography of Jane Austen*. Oxford: Clarendon Press, 1982.

Peter L. DeRose & S. W. McGuire. *A Concordance to the Works of Jane Austen*. New York & London: Garland Publishing, Inc., 1982.

Maggie Lane. *Jane Austen's Family: Through Five Generations.* London: Robert Hale Limited, 1984.

Maggie Lane. *Jane Austen's England.* London: Robert Hale Limited, 1986.

Joan Austen-Leigh. *James Edward Austen-Leigh.* London: The Folio Society Quarterly, 1989.

Joseph Addison. *The Spectator,* No. 112, in The Norton Anthology of British Literature, 7th ed. Vol. 1. New York: W. W. Norton & Co, 2000.

Richard Jenkyns. *A Fine Brush on Ivory: An Appreciation of Jane Austen.* Oxford: Oxford University Press, 2004.

National Portrait Gallery. *Exhibition: Silhouettes.* London: September 2004 - June 2005.